The Educator's Experience of
Pathological Demand Avoidance

by the same illustrator

The Family Experience of PDA
An Illustrated Guide to Pathological Demand Avoidance
Eliza Fricker
ISBN 978 1 78775 677 9
eISBN 978 1 78775 678 6

of related interest

The Panda on PDA
A Children's Introduction to Pathological Demand Avoidance
Glòria Durà-Vilà
Illustrated by Rebecca Tatternorth
ISBN 978 1 83997 006 1
eISBN 978 1 83997 007 8

The Teacher's Introduction to Pathological Demand Avoidance
Essential Strategies for the Classroom
Clare Truman
ISBN 978 1 78775 487 4
eISBN 978 1 78775 488 1

The Educator's Experience of Pathological Demand Avoidance

An Illustrated Guide to Pathological Demand Avoidance and Learning

Laura Kerbey

Foreword by Barney Angliss
Illustrated by Eliza Fricker

Jessica Kingsley Publishers
London and Philadelphia

First published in Great Britain in 2023 by Jessica Kingsley Publishers
An imprint of Hodder & Stoughton Ltd
An Hachette Company

1

Copyright © Laura Kerbey 2023
Foreword copyright © Barney Angliss 2023

The right of Laura Kerbey to be identified as the Author of the Work has been
asserted by her in accordance with the Copyright, Designs and Patents Act 1988.

Front cover images source: Eliza Fricker.

A CIP catalogue record for this title is available from the
British Library and the Library of Congress

ISBN 978 1 83997 696 4
eISBN 978 1 83997 698 8

Printed and bound in the United States by Integrated Books International

Jessica Kingsley Publishers' policy is to use papers that are natural,
renewable and recyclable products and made from wood grown in
sustainable forests. The logging and manufacturing processes are expected
to conform to the environmental regulations of the country of origin.

Jessica Kingsley Publishers
Carmelite House
50 Victoria Embankment
London EC4Y 0DZ

www.jkp.com

This book is dedicated to all the amazing children and young people I have had the pleasure of working with over the last 21 years. Thank you for making my time in education so much fun and for teaching me more about neurodiversity and myself than any other source. Particular thanks go to HPW and AS, for always making me look forward to Mondays.

To my beautiful boys, James and Fin, for being simply the best humans I have ever met and for making me so proud every day. Your time in education was not easy or straightforward, but your determination, courage and humour have always shone and made you into the wonderful young men you are today.

To my mum and dad, you are the best. Thank you for everything you have done for me over the years.

And, finally, to my husband Steve, for being there through the rough and the smooth and for always encouraging me and supporting me in your own, unique way. I know you are proud of me, even though you rarely tell me you are!

Note on the Text

Throughout this book I have referred to "learners with PDA" or "PDAers" and both are used interchangeably. Many neurodivergent individuals prefer identity first language, for example an autistic person will refer to themselves as such, rather than being a person "with autism". However, with PDA, there currently does not seem to be a preference and this is reflected by using both identity first and person first language throughout the book.

Contents

Foreword by Barney Angliss

I'm delighted to be re-acquainted with Laura through this concise and common-sensical book which brings practical advice and huge encouragement to the challenge of parenting, teaching and supporting young people with Pathological Demand Avoidance.

The book comes at a unique and salient time in education: as a result of the COVID-19 pandemic, we all now have experience of education interrupted, education online, education self-monitored, education without walls. Good and bad, enforced learning from home was a hugely novel and still somehow social experiment between 2020 and 2021. For parents whose children experience school-based anxiety and for those who were already home educators by choice or necessity because their child's needs had not been met by the system, this was a moment like no other in which the playing field of education debate became a little more level. Sharing some struggles with these families, parents of children with PDA still have other, very distinct challenges. As Laura highlights in her first chapter, around 70 per cent of children with PDA were already unable to tolerate their school environment or were home educated long before the pandemic; however, the very confusing characteristics of extreme demand avoidance require a more complete re-think of the learning process and of the relationship between educator and child. Laura rightly describes as essential the ability to think on one's feet, to turn plans inside out in order to connect with PDA.

For some years, Laura has provided expert guidance to schools and families, now distilling her observations into this simple volume. The clarity of her notes and the lightness of her style are no surprise to me. Although I had for some time known of Laura by reputation as an experienced leader in specialist education for neurodiverse children – experience with which I myself had quite little to compare – our first proper meeting came in 2016. Talented and subtly confident, Laura was hosting a weekly radio show and invited me to pick some tunes and talk about our work. My original "long list" of suggested tracks unwittingly linked Carole King's "It's Too Late", Moloko's "The Time Is Now" and Fairport Convention's "Who Knows Where the Time Goes?" with Sandy Denny's unforgettable performance completing a trio of female vocalists all concerned with time: time lost, time to come and the unforgiving pressure of the present. If this book had a soundtrack, perhaps those songs would serve equally well for the purpose since time – and the dread of "NOW" – plays significantly in the perplexing presentation of PDA.

Indeed, I've heard from parents that there is no "now" in PDA and then, quite suddenly, it is **all** now. In her excellent chapter on "Weaving in Interests and Learning from Each Other" (Chapter 8), Laura gives two perfect examples of the tension between trying to develop learners' motivation through careful planning and inadvertently denying them the autonomy and spontaneity which they require and which form the humming engine of PDA. The desire for novelty and sparkling, free-flowing self-expression is one of many features which set PDA apart in the handbooks from autism and yet... and yet, we always return to PDA's complicated on-off relationship with autism. Is PDA a version of autism, a subset, an extension, a common bedfellow? Or is it none of these? Whose evidence should we trust on the matter – clinical experts, whose explanations often compete with each other? Or experts-by-experience who are generally the first to recognise that defining PDA is, at best, a quixotic pursuit?

This is not by any means to dismiss clinicians' knowledge or the vast research library now available. These are enormously important to an understanding of the nature of demand avoidance and the impact of PDA on the person who experiences it. But if one is conscious of PDA as the individual's fight for social identity, one must be alert to the danger of *imposing* a diagnostic pattern rather than forming one from observation and interaction with the individual.

That's why, on picking up Laura's text, I'm at once struck by how faithfully she seeks to tell the stories of young people and how delicately she balances these with caution and with theory. This is a book which wastes no words nor seeks to draw more from any one exemplar than is wholly justified. Charmingly illustrated by Eliza Fricker, *The Educator's Experience of PDA* is a vibrant, authentic and energising insight from Laura's years of working with these remarkable young people.

Acknowledgements

Thank you to my friend Eliza for her beautiful illustrations for this book, I don't know how you do it but everything you draw captures my thoughts so perfectly. It has been a pleasure working together on this book which is a testimony to what two neurodivergent brains can achieve.

Thank you to my "Neurodivergent Squad" for all your support and advice, not just for me but for the countless families you work so hard for, and your tireless efforts to make the world of SEN and Education a better place to be.

Finally, thank you to my editor at JKP for all your help in fulfilling my lifetime ambition to write a book.

Introduction

H i, I'm Laura, I am an education and autism consultant with a special interest in pathological demand avoidance (PDA) and I am starting this book with a couple of confessions

---

Confession No 1

PDA used to scare me.

Many years ago, I started a new job at a specialist school. I already had eight years of specialist teaching under my belt, a postgrad in autism and I was a Surrey Autism Champion.

There were a handful of students in this new school who were unlike any others I had worked with. They perplexed me, intrigued me, frustrated, baffled me and, at times, scared me. I thought I knew about autism but these students always seemed to be one step ahead of me.

We had good days when we saw the most incredible, creative, intelligent and caring young people.

We had bad days when lessons were refused and work was ripped up.

And then we had terrible days, when people would get hurt and property would be destroyed.

I used all my tried and tested autism strategies; at best they worked for a day but most of the time they made things worse. I felt deskilled and as if I was failing these students.

I will never forget the "lightbulb moment" I experienced when I first read about PDA.

I realised **everything** I was doing was wrong.

I needed to learn.

I needed to change.

I worked in an environment where so many students needed structure, routine, rewards and predictability.

But these students needed novelty, they needed spontaneity, they needed control, they needed trust and they needed autonomy.

When I left that school and set up PAST (Positive Autism Support and Training, which later became NEST (Neurodivergent Education Support and Training), I started to meet more and more children with PDA. I continued to "unprogramme" myself from many of the things I had learned about autism and education.

I read everything I could about PDA, **but** I learned the most about PDA from the children I worked with; they are the best teachers I had ever met, and I continue to learn from them all the time.

I now absolutely **love** working with individuals with PDA. It no longer scares me, it fascinates, motivates and inspires me.

Confession No 2
When you work in education you are not supposed to have favourites – but I absolutely do – and they **all** have PDA!!!!

CHAPTER 1

What Is PDA?

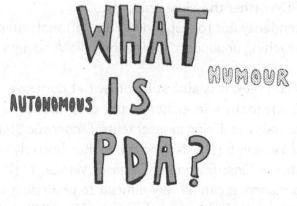

autistic

SENSORY

CHARISMATIC

WHAT

IS

HUMOUR

AUTONOMOUS

PDA?

ANXIOUS

COMMUNICATION

STRONG
INTERESTS

Pathological demand avoidance, also known as PDA, is a type of autism. As well as experiencing the social communication and sensory differences that are present in more "typical" presentations of autism, an individual with PDA will need to avoid demands that are placed upon them or expected of themselves, while also needing to retain control of situations and their environment. As well as sharing these characteristics of autism, the main characteristics of PDA include:

- a need for control, which is often anxiety related
- the drive to avoid everyday demands and expectations (including things that they want to do or enjoy) to an extreme extent
- the tendency to use approaches that are "social in nature" in order to avoid demands
- presentation of many of the key features of PDA rather than just one or two
- tendency not to respond to conventional parenting, teaching or support approaches. (PDA Society n.d.)

PDA is complex. It is also still somewhat controversial as it does not feature in either of the diagnostic manuals professionals use during assessments: *Diagnostic Statistical Manual Version 5* (DSM-5) or the rather horribly named *International Classification of Diseases Version 11* (ICD-11). For this reason, it can be very difficult to get a diagnosis of PDA and most individuals with this profile will likely have a diagnosis of "ASD with a PDA profile" or "autism with high anxiety and demand avoidance" rather than a standalone diagnosis of "pathological demand avoidance".

There is far more to PDA than just demand avoidance, which we all experience at times. Most of us will avoid things that are unappealing, boring, perceived as dangerous or anxiety provoking. To an individual with PDA all demands are perceived as threats to their autonomy and safety and will be rejected or avoided at all costs.

In 2018 the PDA Society conducted a survey of almost 1000 children and young people with a PDA profile. This study, entitled "Being Misunderstood", made for sad and shocking reading. The results of this study, which can be viewed on The PDA Society Website,[1] showed that of 969 young people with PDA who were surveyed 70 per cent were not able to tolerate their school environment or were home educated.

Within the bespoke tutoring company that I co-run, almost all of our students are autistic with a PDA profile. Many of our students have had difficult, negative and even traumatic experiences within the education system but are now thriving with their education otherwise than at school (EOTAS) programmes.

The educational environment is full of demands. Some of them are obvious and include direct demands like:

- Sit down.
- Start your work.
- Stop talking.
- Line up now please.

---

1   https://www.pdasociety.org.uk/wp-content/uploads/2019/08/BeingMisunderstood.pdf

Some demands are less direct and may include more subtle demands such as:

- It's time to start your work now.
- Let's all turn to page seven.
- We need to go to assembly now.

Other demands, such as the following, are more like silent expectations:

- Being polite and using manners.
- Following a timetable.
- Following rules of games.

And, lastly, a learner with PDA is likely to place self-imposed demands on themselves too:

- I must finish my work.
- I should do my work perfectly.
- I must write neatly.

The National Curriculum is, in my opinion, simply too narrow and constrictive for many learners, particularly those with PDA who require autonomy, novelty and spontaneity to thrive.

I don't believe for one moment that learners with PDA don't want to learn. On the contrary they are hungry to learn and hungry for knowledge about new and interesting things. Learners with PDA are more than capable of learning and thriving when given the correct support, understanding and environment and can then meet their potential and achieve great success.

I am still in contact with many of the wonderful students with PDA who I have had the pleasure of working with over the years. Many are now working in brilliant, fulfilling careers including engineering, IT and healthcare. I am also lucky enough to count some adults with PDA amongst my close friends and colleagues. These adults now have very successful careers, most of them self-employed, but all thriving despite their challenging and difficult experiences of school and education.

Let's not forget that if 70 per cent of learners with PDA are not able to tolerate school, then 30 per cent are. There are some amazing schools and educational professionals out there who are getting it right, who are bringing out the best in these bright, charismatic and wonderful students. I hope that, by reading this book, you will have a better, clearer, understanding of these brilliant children and young people, and that this will not only benefit you, but also the students you are lucky enough to work with.

CHAPTER 2

Making Connections

If you are an educational professional reading this book (and if you are I am so grateful that you are doing so, thank you) there are a few really important things you need to know.

Remember that, in any educational setting, reasonable adjustments should be based on **needs** and not diagnosis. Some of the very best schools I have had the pleasure of working with have done incredible work with children with PDA who actually don't have a formal diagnosis. They have simply identified that these children have PDA and have made the necessary adjustments to allow them to thrive in their settings.

- As well as the need to avoid demands and remain in control, PDAers require **autonomy**, which I will talk about later in this book.
- A learner with PDA will not see hierarchy, authority or age, so you **must** present yourself as an equal and someone who they can learn to trust.
- For a learner with PDA to feel safe in any educational setting they **must** have at least one safe

person and a safe place to go when their anxiety gets heightened.
- Everyone with PDA is unique and different. If you are lucky enough to work with more than one learner with PDA, then it is essential that you treat every single one as an individual.
- Any learning environment is going to be difficult for a learner with PDA and it is important to remember that **you** are part of the environment. Your actions, voice, body language and intentions will all alter the environment in a positive or negative way.
- If you are lucky enough to work with a learner with PDA, the most fundamentally important part of your job is to build trust and connection with them.
- You cannot rush this connection, you need to allow it to form genuinely, however long it takes.

Connections **have** to be genuine with a learner with PDA. Trying to force a connection with an individual with PDA is like trying to force two north ends of magnets together. It is physically impossible to make a connection and the two magnets will just keep repelling. However, changing the shape or the orientation of the magnets means that they will pull together and connect.

Some of the children I have worked with have made their best connections with adults in schools who are not education staff. Caretakers who have spent hours of their time with children who are unable to access classrooms, allowing them to potter around the school and help them with fixing things or painting fences, have been invaluable "safe people" for learners with PDA. Another child I worked with who was not in school formed a brilliant, trusting connection with the family dog walker. She became his safe person he could talk to about his worries and he happily left the house with her each day to walk and talk together, always returning happier and calmer after spending time with this lovely lady who had never heard of PDA before she met this child.

When you work with a learner with PDA don't think of yourself as a teacher, tutor, learning support assistant (LSA) or teaching assistant (TA), think of yourself as a "learning facilitator". The chances are you are working with a child who is bright and articulate who already has a wealth of knowledge. Many learners with PDA are autodidactic, meaning that they have a true ability to self-teach. Your role is to facilitate their learning, not only by building on that connection but by helping the child see the value in learning in exciting and meaningful ways. You should also allow the learner to become your teacher too, as this will create a truly equal and reciprocal relationship.

During my time working with learners with PDA I have learned so much from them. They have taught me so many interesting and unusual things. I have been taught how to play chess, draw cartoon characters, how to code and how to play some computer games, albeit very badly!

I have always described children with PDA as "adults trapped inside children's bodies". A child with PDA is unlikely see themselves as a child, so they may feel that you are patronising or speaking down to them if you treat them as such.

Remember that individuals with PDA don't see age, hierarchy or authority like a neurotypical child would, so always present yourself as an equal to the child you are working with. A child with PDA I met recently told me he simply could not understand the rules of the secondary school he had attended for just a couple of weeks before it became unbearable for him. "How come teachers get to sit on comfortable chairs when we sit on hard plastic ones?" he asked me. "And why are teachers allowed to shout at children, but if I shouted back

I would get into so much trouble?" This lack of equality and fairness was just completely wrong to this child and was one of the reasons he was unable to tolerate school.

To form a real and genuine connection with a learner with PDA, you must take your time to learn about what they love and are interested in. You cannot rush this connection and must let it evolve at a natural and organic rate. Many children with PDA may have had some negative experiences within the education system so, understandably, it may take them a while to trust you.

I had the pleasure of working with a tiny infant school for the entire time they had a child with PDA with them (almost three years). The head teacher was wonderful and arranged for me to do some staff training before the child started with them in Reception. She told the staff at the start of my training that she did not care if the child picked up a pencil or book for the entire first year that they were with them, and reassured the staff that their primary role was to form a connection with them and ensure that they left each day feeling happy. It wasn't always an easy ride and the child did very little "formal work" for that first year, but they did form amazing connections with the staff and, when they left the school at the end of Year 2, were reading books for eight-year-olds and writing beautifully too.

Some of the best sessions I have had with the children I work with have not involved anything that would be seen as a "formal learning" but have just involved us sitting and chatting about their special interests. So enjoy this time together and see it as equally valuable as any formal lesson. The stronger the connection, the higher the trust. The higher the trust, the lower their anxiety will be. The lower their anxiety, the higher their demand tolerance will become.

Plus, PDAers are some of the most interesting, funny, entertaining people I have ever met, so why wouldn't you just want to hang out and chat with them?!

CHAPTER 3

The Antidote to Anxiety Is Trust

A lovely parent once told me that they thought, "the opposite of anxiety is trust", which I loved, but then slightly adapted to "the antidote to anxiety is trust" and this is so, so true for a child with PDA.

An individual with PDA has to feel autonomous in any situation. If you take away their autonomy then their anxiety will increase and their demand tolerance will decrease.

I actually prefer the terms "pervasive drive for autonomy" coined by Tomlin Wilding, or "persistent drive for autonomy" coined by Dr Wenn Lawson in describing PDA. There is so much more to PDA than just demand avoidance and I prefer these acronyms, first because they sound more positive. Second, because I feel they are more accurate in describing the need for freedom from demands and control of others that an individual with PDA experiences.

Whichever acronym you prefer, you must always remember the heightened anxiety an individual with PDA will feel if demands are placed upon them and their autonomy is taken away.

A really helpful analogy to use here is the "bucket analogy". Imagine a bucket with holes in it. This represents the bucket of a neurotypical individual. Throughout the day everyone must deal with stress, sensory issues, demands etc. These little things gradually "fill the bucket" but, when there are holes in the bucket, the stresses and anxiety can drain away, so it takes something very big or unusual for the bucket to fill up.

Contrarily, the PDA bucket does not have any holes in it. Also, the baseline of anxiety for an individual with PDA is much, much higher than the baseline of a neurotypical child. This means that the bucket already has less capacity, but it also has no holes in it, so the bucket just keeps filling up every time the individual has to face a demand, a sensory difference or a social communication difficulty etc. As a result, it does not take much for the bucket to fill up and overspill. This is when the individual with PDA will go into crisis, meltdown or shutdown.

When we work with learners with PDA it is essential that we identify their "bucket fillers" and their "bucket emptiers". If we can reduce the fillers and increase the "emptiers" we can reduce the rate at which the bucket fills up and thus reduce the chance of it reaching its capacity.

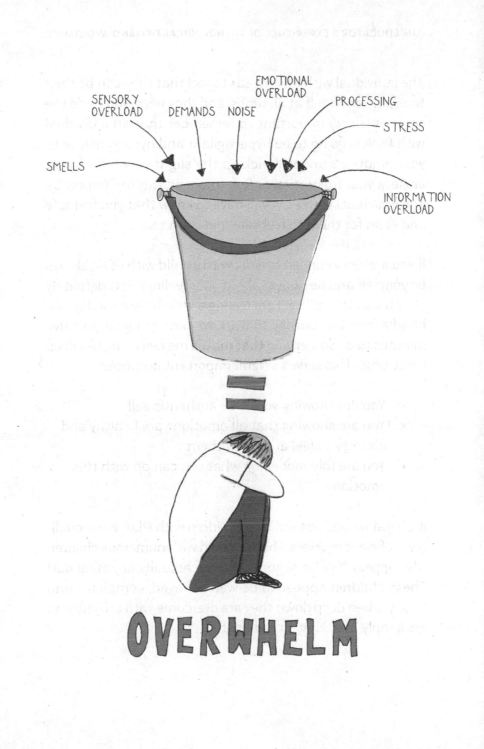

The individual with PDA needs to feel that they can be their true, authentic self at all times, and they need **you** to do the same. It is very important to remember that an individual with PDA is going to be hypervigilant and hypersensitive to your emotions and will pick up the slightest whiff of your anxiety, your frustration or fear (more on this in Chapter 5). The individual with PDA will have to know that you feel safe and calm for them to feel safe and calm too.

If you are lucky enough to work with a child with PDA, always be yourself and be honest about your feelings. It is definitely okay to say things like "I am feeling a little bit stressed today. I had a horrible journey to work so I am going to take five minutes to do something that makes me feel calm, like deep breathing." This serves several important purposes:

- You are showing your true authentic self.
- You are showing that all emotions are healthy and it's okay to feel and show them.
- You are role modelling what you can do with this emotion.

It is vital we understand that children with PDA are incredibly proficient maskers. I have worked with numerous children who appear "fine in school" who are actually anything but! These children appear to be well behaved, compliant and happy, when deep down they are overcome with anxiety and are simply "masking" or hiding it.

These are the children who then "implode" or "explode" when back with their safe people or in the safe place: parents, car, home. Sadly, many parents who are in this predicament are not always believed and some are even blamed for their child's behaviour.

This phenomenon is sometimes referred to as "the coke bottle analogy". Imagine a bottle of fizzy drink that has been constantly shaken all day. When you take the lid off that bottle, it is going to explode. To stop the bottle from doing this you would allow it to rest and settle for long enough until the contents are "calm" again. It is vital that children and young people with PDA have the chance to do this upon their return from school, where they are likely to have been "shaken up" all day.

If you work in any educational setting and a parent tells you that their child is really struggling with school, and you feel that they seem "fine" when they are there, please, please do listen to this parent and work with them to help reduce their child's anxiety.

Children with PDA are often socially very savvy. They don't want to look different to their peers so may often sit feeling excruciatingly uncomfortable and anxious rather than ask for help.

This is where your connection with the child will be so important. Not only will you become more proficient at picking up on the signals that the child is anxious (hair twiddling, giggling, blinking, zoning out, humming etc. are just some examples) but you can say things like "Fractions? Yuck! I remember doing them at school and I found them really hard. Shall we try and work them out together?" This language removes the demand to ask for help and allows you to work towards shared goals as equals.

Remember also that children who are anxious do not always "look anxious". I have worked with children who have been accused of being arrogant, bossy and controlling. Once when I was doing an observation of a child in a primary school the special educational needs coordinator (SENCO) pointed out to me that he couldn't be anxious as he was "walking round the playground like he owned it!" What she was failing to see was that this child was masking, his strutting around the playground was a way of protecting himself from the demands of socialising and communicating with other children.

I have also worked with several children who sing when they are anxious at school, which has also been misread as defiance or deliberately disruptive behaviour. Singing can be a type of "stim" or self-stimulating behaviour which can both soothe and block out the environment. Being prevented from singing or humming can actually raise anxiety to unbearable levels.

Anxiety can also look like other emotions such as anger, sadness, frustration or shyness.

Anxious

Anxious

Anxious

Anxious

It can be really helpful to allow a learner with PDA to have a "soft start" in the morning, allowing them to come into school and go to a safe place, such as the library, where they can read or draw until their anxiety levels are low enough for them to enter the classroom.

Some children I have worked with have also enjoyed having responsibilities they can engage in at the start of the day. One lovely little boy I worked with struggled daily with attending his primary school, until he was given the role of "eco-warrior", a high-viz jacket, a "grabby stick" and a badge which he wore with pride. Each morning he would come into school, still anxious, but instead of having to go straight into the classroom and face the demands that posed, he happily went into the playground and collected all the litter he could find, then came into the classroom when he was ready, his "bucket" less full and more able to cope with the demands of the day. Another child I worked with enjoyed coming in each morning and doing a "treasure hunt" around the school grounds which was linked to his favourite computer game, again this low-demand, fun activity helped greatly with the anxiety of the school day, and allowed him to integrate into the day when he was ready.

Other children I have worked with have enjoyed going to work in younger children's classes in the morning, listening to them read or helping adults in the school with various jobs. Any ideas such as these must be created with full input and collaboration of the learner so that they see these as "shared goals" and must not be presented as yet another demand. The novelty of such roles and responsibilities may not last long but could be extremely helpful in supporting the child and ensuring they feel valued and included within their educational provision.

A "check out" with a trusted person at the end of the day provides an opportunity to discuss anything positive or challenging that has happened that day and can also help to reduce anxiety about what is happening the following day.

An important note on which to finish this chapter is that a lot of focus is placed on "emotional regulation" for learners with PDA, but before a person can regulate their emotions it is important to ensure that they can recognise them.

I had the pleasure of working with a lovely college student with PDA a few years ago. She and I were chatting about anxiety during a session. I was explaining to her what anxiety was, its function and ways that we could recognise when our anxiety was on the rise and techniques to help manage and reduce it. She looked at me in complete surprise and said "I just thought this was how everyone felt all the time!" She had spent 18 years of her life in a state of perpetual anxiety and did not realise there was another way for her to feel. So before we even start to try and teach "emotional regulation" we have to begin with "emotional recognition" and talking about your own emotions: when you feel them, and what can help you is a good place to begin. A really good speech language therapist or occupational therapist with knowledge and understanding of PDA can be a vital part of the team in supporting a learner with this important concept too.

CHAPTER 4

The Importance of Humour

Two of the most important characteristics to possess when you work with children and teens with PDA are a good sense of humour and a thick skin!

The children with PDA I have worked with have all had wonderful, unique senses of humour and enjoyed having a laugh, sometimes at my expense!

Humour is a great leveller and, as I have already explained in Chapter 3, it is essential to a PDAer that they feel you are on the same level as them as they just don't see authority or hierarchy.

This need for equality means that sometimes you may be the butt of the joke. Remember that this is not down to a lack of respect but the inability to see authority and you need to take this on the chin!

Sharing a sense of humour and silly jokes will demonstrate to a child with PDA that you value the relationship with them more than the need for them to do "work or learning" and can be extremely helpful in building that essential connection.

Humour relieves tension and can be a great distractor during times of high anxiety. Using humour tells the PDAer, "It's okay, there's nothing too serious going on here, we can still have a laugh and a joke."

It is an important consideration that an individual with PDA doesn't ever feel that you are laughing at them, particularly during times of high anxiety, so this does need to be gauged carefully.

I once received a message from the parents of a child I worked with to tell me that they were having a really difficult morning and I needed to ensure we had a really low demand session.

I arrived at the session to be greeted by a very unhappy boy who was curled up on the sofa. Eventually he looked at me and exclaimed, "Urgh! What is that on your jacket?!" Looking down I noticed that I had a smearing of something brown on the lapel of my jacket. "This..." I explained, "is Jabba the Hutt's poo..."

Instantly, the tension seemed to lift! We then proceeded to have a ridiculous and very funny conversation about how Jabba the Hutt couldn't wipe his own bum as his arms were too short and that being Jabba's "Butt Wiper" was probably one of the worst jobs in the Galaxy!!

After we stopped laughing, we were able to begin a successful low demand session and when I left my client was feeling much happier.

(And in case you are wondering, it wasn't really Jabba the Hutt's poo, it was chocolate icing from a cake I had carried a couple of days before. But that client and I do sometimes wonder which unfortunate character has the job of wiping Jabba's butt!)

CHAPTER 5

Nonverbal Language – the Silent Trigger!

D ue to their high anxiety learners with PDA are hypervigilant and hypersensitive to their environment, and that includes the people in it.

Individuals with PDA may easily misinterpret emotions, which is why it is so important to be open and honest about them. I have worked with many parents who have said that their child with PDA has accused them of shouting when they have not been. Parents and teachers have also commented that children with PDA have asked them why they are "cross" or "angry" when the parent has actually felt mild frustration or stress.

A slight sigh of frustration or "look" between two members of staff is very likely to be picked up on by the learner with PDA, which will increase their anxiety enormously.

Think of a smoke detector that is far, far too sensitive to the environment and goes off every time someone walks down your street with a cigarette. That is how sensitive the child with PDA could be to the people in the environment around them.

Many children with PDA I have worked with will tell me that they don't like their teacher or TA because they are "too strict" or "too shouty". Their neurotypical peers may just feel that their teacher is a little on the firm side, but to the learner with PDA this teacher could be utterly terrifying!

I once worked with a girl with PDA who had two LSAs supporting her at school, one in the mornings and one in the afternoons. She loved one of them but found the other very hard to be with. She found it very hard to articulate what it was about the one she didn't like but just said she was "strict" or "bossy". When I met the two LSAs I could tell instantly which was which. They were both lovely, but while one was warm and positive and clearly really enjoyed just being with this girl and letting learning evolve naturally, the other seemed more focused on formal learning and progress. The girl had worked this out and quite simply recognised the agenda of the second LSA, which she found far more demanding and therefore anxiety provoking too.

It is really important to be aware of your body language, tone of voice and facial expressions when working with learners with PDA as they are very likely to see or sense if you are not feeling calm and relaxed. Your emotions will not only be picked up on but likely exaggerated in their perception.

This is why honesty is always the best policy with a child with PDA.

I once arrived at a school to work with one of my clients with PDA. I had had a very difficult morning as my own son was very unwell at the time. I tried to "be professional" and hide my anxiety, but within minutes of starting my session with this boy he asked me if I was okay. I explained that my son was unwell and that I was quite worried about him and would probably have to take him to hospital when I finished work. The child said in a very sincere manner that he was sorry to hear that and hoped my son would be alright. Some may argue that I had been unprofessional or allowed boundaries to blur in sharing this information with this child, but if I had lied and said everything was "fine" he would have sensed that it was not, and this could have been potentially damaging to the trust we had built up. The boy may have also worried that he had done something to make me feel upset, and this would have really increased his anxiety too. Obviously, it is important to keep professional boundaries and not share information that could be inappropriate, but when working with a learner with PDA it is essential to protect your relationship and connection with them at all times.

CHAPTER 6

The Power of Choices

Individuals with PDA always require autonomy around their learning and during times of raised anxiety may become more controlling as they feel their autonomy slipping away. By carefully offering choices when working with learners with PDA we can help them feel that they have retained the essential values of autonomy and control.

Rather than giving direct demands to a learner with PDA it is far more appropriate and effective to offer them a choice. Here are some examples:

Instead of "You need to start your maths now" you could ask the following:

- "Would you like to start with this task or this task?"
- "Would you like to work with me in the classroom or shall we find a quiet space in the library?"
- "How many questions do you think you can get done?"

You may of course receive the following replies to these questions: "Neither!" or "none!" and that is okay. You could then reply with "Yes, those questions do look a bit boring don't they. Perhaps we can go on the iPad and find another way to work on this instead?"

During the first lockdown I was supporting a lovely boy with PDA with online sessions. At the end of one session he asked me if I could create a quiz on Aztecs and Incas for us to do together the next time we met. I said I would happily do that and that I looked forward to doing the quiz with him the following week.

Quiz prepared and ready I logged on for our next session and told the boy that I was ready with the quiz, upon which a look of pure horror and panic came over his face. I am not sure if he had forgotten, or if the demand to do the quiz was too much for him that day, but I thought he was going to slam his laptop shut. "It's fine!" I reassured him, "We don't have to do the quiz today, or we can give it a go but with a twist. You can offer me the right answer or a silly answer!" This gave this boy the autonomy to try the quiz without any pressure and he agreed to give it a go. If he knew the answer to the question, he could impress me with his (vast) knowledge of Ancient American history or, if he didn't know the answer, he could make me laugh. This became a win/win situation for us both and the quiz session turned out to be a great success.

The same child and I were once discussing the fact that if you only ever gave the answer "Paris" to any question you were asked during your entire time in education, one day you would be right. "The answer is Paris!" became our catchphrase for some time, and again meant that if I ever asked him something to which he didn't know the answer he could answer with this phrase, which always sent us both into fits of giggles.

I think one of my favourite choices to offer is that of "time or support": asking a learner "Would you like some time to work on this yourself?" or "Would you like me to work on this with you?" This choice gives the learner the autonomy they need, while also supporting and gently encouraging their independence.

When working with learners with PDA I always have a wide range of activities, tasks and games to offer them. I allow them to rummage through my bag of resources and choose what they would like to do. Sometimes nothing I have to offer is enough to entice them but they themselves will have their own ideas of what they want to do, and then we proceed with that activity. I would never dream of starting a session with a learner with PDA with the words "This is what we are doing today", as this would be perceived as an instant demand.

It is important to remember that just offering someone a choice will not automatically guarantee that one will be picked. I recall a child with PDA telling me about the choices that he was being offered at school, "They may as well ask me if I want to play with a Barbie doll or a Cindy doll – I don't want to play with either!" he told me. So choices still need to ensure that the learner feels that they are retaining their autonomy.

Making a choice could also be perceived as a demand and offering too many choices could well overwhelm and lead to panic, so only offer a choice of two things.

To work effectively with learners with PDA it is essential that you can think outside the box, pluck ideas out of thin air and just "go with the flow". I have to be honest and admit that when I first starting working with learners with PDA this felt like it went against everything I had been taught in my teacher training when there is so much pressure to plan and prepare, but now I find it such a lovely, liberating way of working and I cannot imagine doing it any other way!

CHAPTER 7

Wondering, Learning Together and Sharing Demands...

I spend a lot of time "wondering" when I am working with learners with PDA. I will often say things like "I wonder what that would look like if we did it that way?" or "I wonder what would happen if we tried this?" These must be genuine questions so that the learner and I can work together to find things out.

Remember, as mentioned in Chapter 1, that you must not see yourself as a "teacher", "tutor", "TA" or "LSA" but as a "learning facilitator" who has an equal and reciprocal relationship with the child. Working together on tasks cements this role in place and is also really good fun! If I ask a learner with PDA to do a task, I will either do the same task simultaneously or share the task and do it with them. This will not only promote equality but also make the demand of the task seem smaller as it is shared.

When you are working on things together you are also working towards a shared goal, and this is essential in maintaining trust and connections.

Some learners with PDA may enjoy challenges, games and races. These are all great ways to learn together but it is important that the adult in the case is genuinely invested in the challenge, race or game. For example, I may say to a learner with PDA, "I bet I can finish this before you!" when we are working together on something, or "I will race you to the garden" if we are taking our session outside. Then I genuinely try and finish the work before them or get to the garden before them so they can see that the "end goal" is as important to me as it is to them.

CHAPTER 8

Weaving in Interests and Learning from Each Other

U sing the interests of learners with PDA can increase the "What's in it for me?" factor for them while supporting their learning. A child may see the value in reading if it means that they can read computer game instructions better. They may see the value in writing if it means they can write a persuasive letter or email to someone to explain why they need something to be purchased for them. (One of my clients recently wrote me a brilliant letter explaining why they needed me to purchase them an axolotl as part of their EOTAS programme!) They may see the value of maths if it means that they can learn to tell the time or the value of money if this also benefits them in some way. All these things that are taught in school or as part of an EOTAS programme **have** to have meaning and value to the learner with PDA.

A learner with PDA is likely to see many learning tasks as pointless or irrelevant and forcing apparently meaningless tasks upon them will take away their autonomy. It is important for learners to see the point in learning, so that it actually benefits their autonomy rather than diminishing it.

It can be very helpful to use a learner's interests to help facilitate their learning, but some words of caution here:

First, the interests of an individual with PDA are often transient and change regularly. Once, when I started working with a new child, he spent our entire first session talking to me about *Star Wars*. The aim of my sessions with this child was to support him with his emotional recognition and regulation. I have a fairly good knowledge of this subject from my own childhood, so went home and spent hours creating some new *Star Wars* resources, (By the way it is not easy to find pictures of *Star Wars* "baddies" looking anything but "angry!") When I excitedly returned to meet this child for our second session, I proudly produced my brand new resources, only for him to glance at them and tell me that he was not interested in *Star Wars* anymore and proceeded to tell me all about *Knights*!

Second, it is also essential that you do not "hijack" a learner with PDA's interests. Once a client of mine was starting at a new alternative provision who had been told by her parents that she loved Anime. The girl arrived on her first day to be presented with all her work linked to the subject she loved and was mortified that "her" special interest was now being used to make her learn. It can be a tricky balance to reach, but it is vital that you respect the learner's interest and learn **with** them about it, weaving in those learning opportunities rather than tainting something they love with demands and "sneaking" in learning with disingenuous interest in their special interest.

Third, we should always see the value in any of our learners' interests, even those that may be considered "inappropriate" for the learning environment, such as gaming or controversial topics. We still need to show interest and value such topics as they could be your "way in" to making essential connections with these learners and gives you a vital starting point. I once worked with a LSA who was horrified that the child she was supporting was fascinated by dictators, who I pointed out were not only interesting from a historical point of view but from a psychological one too.

I myself scored a huge "own goal" when supporting a young person at a specialist school. This student was unable to access any lessons or do any work he was presented with, instead choosing to be in a room on their own with an LSA. I would frequently check in on the student to see how he was doing, and on one occasion they showed me clay figures of animation characters he had made. This student had many talents and art was one of them. My brain started whirring and I tried to think of ways to use this interest to create some learning experiences. I suggested that he could use this talent to create "models made to order", and the student agreed. I thought that this enterprise could fulfil many learning objectives including numeracy and literacy. The student initially seemed motivated by this idea and went out with their LSA to purchase resources. They designed some posters that they stuck up around the school advertising their wares. Within a day this young person had their first order and I mentally congratulated myself for my brilliant idea. Later that day there was a knock on my office door, and the student's LSA stuck her head around it and said to me "Er, we need you upstairs". As I walked through the school, I saw several posters the student had stuck up ripped off walls and discarded on the floor and, when I entered the room, I was met with a scene reminiscent of a model shop that had been burgled. There was clay and other materials strewn across the floor and, sitting in the corner, was a very upset student. Eventually, he spoke to me, and told me he no longer wanted to make any models. When I asked "Why not?" the student simply looked at me and said "Because you f**cking want me to!" I had not only turned this student's enjoyable activity into "work" but I had also unwittingly placed them under pressure to perform and taken away their autonomy too.

The learner with PDA simply must see the intrinsic value in learning for them to be able to willingly undertake it, because even our own desire for them to complete a task or our enthusiasm over their interest can create a demand.

A few years ago I was working with a family who had a

15-year-old son with a PDA profile. When I began working with him he was not attending school and, despite the regular reminders from the adults around him that he "had to get his maths and English GCSE", had no interest or motivation to engage in these subjects as he just did not see the point. A few months later this boy went to stay with a family friend who was a mechanic. He really enjoyed helping out in the workshop and the manual work he was undertaking. He spoke to one of the other mechanics about how he could get into this type of work himself and was told that he would need to go to college and would require a qualification in maths or English to do so. This was the "what's in it for me" factor that was required for this boy to phone his parents and tell them that he "needed to get his maths and English" as he was now able to see the point or value in these qualifications which had just seemed pointless and arbitrary beforehand. I am pleased to say that this boy did indeed get these qualifications!

The beauty of working with learners with PDA is that you never quite know where the learning journey is going to take you. One of the best sessions I have had with one of my regular PDA clients was about Guy Fawkes on a warm summer's day in his garden. I had no idea we would be learning about Guy Fawkes when I arrived at his house that morning, but when we had been chatting for a while, the conversation took us on this path. We ended up re-enacting the Gunpowder Plot using lots of his cuddly toys, with Guy Fawkes being played by a toy fox, and renamed "Guy Fox" in a stroke of pure genius by the child. We used my phone to look up historical facts and by the end of the 90-minute session both of us had learned so much about the politics, royalty and other lesser known facts about this time in history.

INTERESTS

GET TO KNOW...

SPEND TIME

SHOW GENUINE INTEREST

ASK ABOUT

Another time I arrived at a client's house to work with their son and the first thing he asked me was "Laura, did you know that there is a type of fish that fight with their penis?!". My response was "No! But I would love to hear all about it and would love you to teach me more!" and I left an hour later fully clued up on Persian Carpet worms and their rather fascinating fighting habits! (Google them – they are very interesting creatures!!)

On another occasion I arrived at a school to meet a client and was informed by his TA that he was having a very bad morning. When I went to meet the child he was indeed having a very difficult time and informed me that he was going to "chop off my head" and those of the other adults trying to calm him down. "Ah!" I said, "You sound like Henry VIII!" "Who was he?" the boy asked, so I started to talk about Henry and his penchant for decapitating those who had fallen from his favour. His interest piqued the boy and I decided to go to the library and ended up having a brilliant session all about Henry VIII, his many wives and the gorier aspects of his reign. That evening I received a lovely email from the boy's mum telling me that her son had come home and excitedly told her all about his new favourite king: "I didn't know you would be teaching him history!" the mum wrote, and I replied "Neither did I!"

I think the best way to describe the perfect learning environment for a learner with PDA would be to use the analogy of a market.

- The marketplace would be full of stalls displaying an eclectic range of tempting and exciting items and goods.

- Learners would be allowed to browse the market-place at their leisure and in their own time.
- Learners would be able to pick up and try items without committing to "buying them".
- Stalls could be visited as many times as the child liked, and things could be tried and tested as many times as needed before the child made a decision.
- Stall holders would be friendly, open and patient. They would be passionate about what they were selling and join in with demonstrations and trying goods out.
- Stall holders running the market stalls would engage and connect with the children without putting any pressure on anyone to commit or "buy".
- Items could be "returned" if the child changed their mind or didn't want to complete a purchase – without judgement from the stall holders.

Now, if I am being really honest here, this analogy is far easier to replicate when a learner has EOTAS or one to one support in a learning environment. I understand that this model of education is much, much harder to replicate in mainstream settings, particularly the secondary system in the UK.

Unfortunately, I meet many learners with PDA who just about managed in primary school who have then found the transition into secondary school incredibly challenging, many of them becoming too anxious to continue attending or requiring alternative placements at this stage of their education. There are many reasons for this. The secondary school system is much less autonomous than the primary system; there are a far greater number of transitions to cope with each day, a far greater number of students to interact with, increased homework and sensory overwhelm.

That said, I have worked with some secondary schools that have done some great work with learners with PDA, but I do feel that the necessary reasonable adjustments are much, much harder to implement in this phase of education.

I have also worked with some learners with PDA who have "bypassed" a traditional secondary school, and then transitioned into colleges where they have been able to focus their learning on the subjects they love and dropped the many subjects they see as pointless or arbitrary. Within the further education system their autonomy has been retained to some degree.

"You will be asKed questions you have never been
asKed before and have conversations you could
never predict."

CHAPTER 9

Praise and Rewards

Most teachers and educational professionals will naturally praise the success of the learner they work with. Before I started working with learners with PDA I would always use a lot of praise to reinforce learning and "good behaviour". The first time I enthusiastically said, "Good boy!" to a boy I was working with he looked at me in disgust and told me "I am not a dog!"

Praise needs to be delivered very carefully when working with learners with PDA and there are various reasons for this.

First, praise could be perceived as patronising. Remember that the learner with PDA sees themselves as your equal, so praising them could feel like you are putting yourself in a position that is above them.

Second, praising a child for "conforming with a demand" such as completing their work could set up an expectation that this demand would now be met again. The fact that the child has completed a task and is then praised for it could raise their anxiety significantly so that they then feel too anxious to try it again.

Third, if you praise publicly this could make the learner feel that they have been "put on the spot" and attention focused on them, which could feel extremely uncomfortable for them and again cause a surge in anxiety.

So it is important to exercise extreme caution when praising, which can feel quite alien at first if it is something you are used to doing. Rather than saying "Well done for completing your work", you could try instead reflecting on what it is you like about the work, such as the colours in a picture or the wording in a story.

When you have built up a good, solid and trusting connection with a learner with PDA you could use humour to praise in a fun and indirect way too. This is particularly relevant when you are working on tasks together.

FLEXIBLE

HUMOUR

LESS PRESSURE

You can also let children overhear you talking about them in a genuine and honest way to others.

LIGHTNESS = LESS EXPECTATION = LESS DEMAND

Another really important point for those who work with learners with PDA who find school very hard: **Don't praise them for coming in to school!** I have worked with many children and young people who find attending school extremely difficult, so it is only natural that, when they do attend, the adults supporting them praise them for being there. This can cause so much anxiety and embarrassment that it could stop the child from attending again.

The traditional rewards and sanction systems so commonly used in learning environments can cause increased anxiety for learners with PDA. Similarly, some learners with PDA are just not motivated by the approaches that may work for neurotypical or "typically" autistic learners.

I have worked with children and young people who are simply not motivated by house points, merits or certificates. One parent I worked with went into school on her son's last day to help clear out his tray and found more than ten certificates stuffed into it. Her son had no interest in receiving certificates and to him they were just pointless pieces of paper.

For a learner with PDA rewards need to be meaningful and valuable. One child I worked with loved being timed running around the playground. During each lesson he accumulated "minutes" for doing his work, answering questions etc., then, at the end of the lesson, he used these minutes to run around outside and would try and beat his previous times. He could also choose a friend to take outside with him by "sharing his minutes" and this worked well for him for some time.

Once, when I was observing a child with PDA at school, he told me through his tears how much he hated the new "behaviour" system the school had introduced. It was a very public way of displaying which children were doing well and which were not. I am afraid I really don't agree with or approve of these systems for any children but, for a learner with PDA, these are an absolute "**No!**" Can you imagine how anxious it would make you as an adult if you came into work each day to see your performance, good or bad, displayed for all your colleagues to see?

Traditional autism resources and approaches such as "Now/ Next Boards" or "When you have done this then you can do X" can be perceived as demands by a learner with PDA. Instead use "natural consequences" such as "It's great you have tried so hard with this task, you have time to go on the iPad now. Which game would you like to play?" or "You have finished that quickly. You have some free time now, what shall we do in the playground?" or similar. This approach grants the learner the autonomy they need while recognising their achievements in a respectful and natural way.

If a child you are working with is a learner who needs a visual timetable, ensure they have some say and autonomy around this. Rather than presenting it as "this is what you are doing today", which will be perceived as a demand, allow the learner the opportunity to choose the order in which they do things or personalise it using the things in which they are interested. You can always staple on things that cannot be moved, like lunchtime or therapy sessions, but still allow some autonomy around these too. "We can walk to your speech therapy session, or we could jump like a kangaroo!"

CHAPTER 10

Reducing Pressure and Picking Your Battles

When you work with learners with PDA there are two things of which you must always be aware.

First, how anxious is the learner feeling? Remember, the higher an individual's anxiety the lower their demand tolerance will be, and the lower their anxiety the higher their demand tolerance will be.

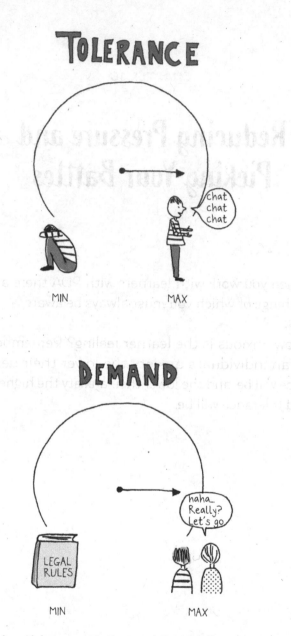

Synchronising expectation and the child's tolerance will always need to be assessed and gauged.

There will be some days when the learner feels able to manage lots of demands and seems able to comply with many of the expectations placed upon them in the learning environment, but the following day it could be a completely different story. It can almost be as if the demand tolerance has been used up, so the following day there is simply none left to be able to cope with further demands. This is "par for the course" when working with PDAers and, on these days, it is important not to see this as a step backwards or a failure on anyone's part. On these days it is essential to implement a low demand approach and focus on retaining relationships and connections. Days when demands have not been tolerated should not be seen as failures, and it is important here to remember how sensitive a learner with PDA is to your feelings and emotions.

Remember the bucket analogy in Chapter 3? As I have already mentioned, this is essential to bear in mind when working with learners with PDA. There will be days when their bucket is just too full to cope with demands and we need to let the bucket sit and rest so that some of the contents (i.e. anxiety) can evaporate or dissipate.

Another essential question to ask yourself when you are supporting learners with PDA is "How necessary is it that this demand is complied with?" or "Does this really matter?"

HOW IMPORTANT IS IT?

Once I was observing a child in school who had taken her shoes and socks off. The child was sitting at her desk working when her teacher came over with her shoes and socks and asked her TA to ask her to put them on. Her TA looked at me for guidance and I mouthed the word "No" to her. I was not wanting to undermine the teacher in any way and at that moment it was simply not necessary for the girl to stop working and put her shoes and socks on. When the bell went for break time it **did** become necessary as it was winter and cold and wet in the playground, and the girl could also have hurt her feet if she was running around outside with bare feet.

On another occasion when I was observing a child with PDA the TA supporting him reminded him that he must "write the learning objective and date, and draw a margin in his book" before he started his work. At being told this, the child put his pencil down and put his head on the desk. Again, this demand was not necessary. The TA could have simply done this for him and removed this barrier so the child could start his work.

There are lots of demands placed on learners in schools that cause unnecessary anxiety. So ask yourself questions like:

- Do they really need to go to assembly?
- Do they really need to write this themselves or can I scribe for them?
- Do they really need to get changed for PE?
- Do they really need to say "please and thank you?"
- Do they really need to finish a piece of work?

All of these things could be filling the bucket unnecessarily, reducing the capacity for more important demands.

One demand with which many of the children and young people I work with really struggle is the demand of doing homework. I have been told on numerous occasions by parents I work with that their child spends more time arguing about homework than the time it would take to do it.

One of my favourite comments ever from a child I worked with was, "Being told to come off my X-Box and do my homework is like having an ice-cream taken off me and having broccoli shoved in my mouth!"

I think we really need to ask if homework is a necessity, as learners with PDA will simply not have the capacity to complete it when they are back in the safety of their homes after school. I have been told by many autistic and PDA children over the years that "schoolwork is for school" and that it does not belong in the home environment. I have also worked with children and young people who have been so anxious about not doing their homework that they have been unable to go back to school as they are so worried about the consequences.

Of course there will be times when demands must be complied with, but many of these are linked to safety of the child or others and will be discussed later in this book.

"Tenacity!! He has a great ability to focus and research something from start to finish and never give up until he's learnt all there is to learn. The recall he has for facts of his special interest is phenomenal."
ABLO

CHAPTER 11

Be Flexible Enough to Bend So That Neither of You Breaks

W hen working with learners with PDA it is essential for the adults supporting them to "go with the flow".

When demands placed on an individual take them out of the flow, then anxiety will be increased, and the demands will be avoided.

Many learners with a "typical" presentation of autism require structure, predictability and routine, and the absence of these can cause increased anxiety.

Individuals with PDA require novelty, flexibility and spontaneity while a routine or timetable can be perceived as "silent" demands or expectations that lead the individual away from their "flow". You have to flex and flow with the PDAer, and enjoy the unexpected as it occurs!

Having said this, we must remember that an individual with PDA is autistic. Unexpected change and transitions can cause anxiety and disappointment. I find that most of the learners I support will find unexpected changes to their routine difficult to manage, particularly if taking them out of their "flow" or preventing them from doing the things they enjoy. It is still important to try and keep unexpected change to a minimum, and to give plenty of warning if they cannot be prevented.

Timetables will inevitably change in schools and colleges. Staff absence, special occasions such as Sports Day or Christmas performances are part and parcel of life within educational settings, but these are likely to cause anxiety to the learner with PDA as they too are full of demands. Ensure that you are giving the learner plenty of time to process these changes and that you are still giving them as much information and autonomy as possible around them. For example, you could offer the following choices:

"You could play a part in the Christmas production, or you could help us with the sound backstage."

Or

"You could join in with the races on Sports Day, or you could help us time the runners."

Offering choices like this can ensure that the learner is still included in these events, if they wish to be, but allows them the autonomy they need to take part.

A daily "check in" and "check out" will be invaluable in warning learners of change and discussing any anxiety they have around them too.

As mentioned in the last chapter, it is important to always look for signs of raised anxiety and pick your battles.

I have spent many hours preparing resources for sessions with PDAers, often at the request of the learner themselves, only to be told the next time I saw them that they "don't want to do it today". It would be completely futile for me to explain that I had spent time on the preparation and so I have to accept that we simply won't be using said resources that day and keep them safe for another occasion.

One of my brilliant colleagues once did a session with a mutual client where they spent a lot of time working on learning linked to pirates. A few days later this tutor donned full pirate gear, even walking down the street in full view of rather bemused onlookers, only to be told when he arrived at the boy's house that he did not want to work on anything to do with pirates that day! The tutor spent the whole session dressed as a pirate working on something completely different!

When supporting a child with PDA we must always be on the lookout for raised anxiety or boredom, or signals that work is leading the learner away from their "flow" and react appropriately to this in a way that doesn't cause further anxiety or guilt. If I see that one of my learners is getting bored, becoming frustrated, finding the work too difficult or easy I will make an excuse for them and say something like "This is getting a bit boring now isn't it? Shall we try something else?"

Something else that I have had to teach myself during my time working with learners with PDA is that finishing is not important. Finishing a task can be regarded as another type of demand and can also cause anxiety about the task being "perfect". I literally have dozens of unfinished tasks and pieces of work I have started with my learners, but we have still been able to learn loads together and I have been able to evidence progress through the work that has been completed.

Remember that the interests of an individual with PDA change regularly and you can always revisit learning tasks in the future if the interest or flow returns to this topic.

CONSISTENCY

CHAPTER 12

Blame the Government!

As well as seeking the "What's in it for me?" factor learners with PDA will also need to know "why" they should conform with demands. Using opinions such as "it's dangerous" or "you are too young" simply won't wash with a learner with PDA and you will need to explain the reason for demand compliance using facts (which you may have to embellish a little!) and not opinions.

I once arrived at a school to work with a child with PDA who was less than happy that his break time had been "ruined" as it was "Wet Break". This child explained to me that he liked being outside in the rain and was allowed to play outside at home whatever the weather. I told the boy that it was indeed very annoying that he could not go outside, but that it was beyond the school's control as it was a rule that the government had imposed. Once the boy had a "reason" for his perceived imprisonment he calmed down and stopped directing his anger to the adults who had imposed this rule.

Several years ago I worked with a young person who was phenomenally gifted at IT. Their goal was to go to university to study computer science. The natural progression route from their school was to attend a local college and get the necessary qualifications for them to then attend university. Understandably this learner saw absolutely no value at all in doing a "pointless B-Tech" course as they knew how to do all the work already. I managed to speak to a local university who invited both myself and the boy to have a look around the campus and have lunch with one of the professors. After some initial awkwardness the boy started to open up and chat to the professor about computers and IT. Unfortunately, I had absolutely no idea what they were talking about as I am very "téchnically challenged" but the professor was obviously very impressed with what he heard. The professor genuinely sympathised with the boy's opinions about the B-Tech, but said that, unfortunately, it was something any university would insist on and was a necessary step that anyone who wanted to do a degree would have to take. This amazing professor then offered the student work experience over the entire summer holidays at the university which he attended every day. He then went on to do the B-Tech, then to university and now has a successful career in IT.

CHAPTER 13

Using Empathy and Validation

There will be days when the learner with PDA's anxiety will be too high to comply with any demands, and there may be days when you become the target of their frustration. You may be ignored, sworn at or even hit, but remember that this is coming from a place of extreme anxiety and the learner with PDA may feel deep shame afterwards.

One of the most important things I have learned from PDAers is that, for any individual, there is no such thing as an overreaction. The individual's reaction to a situation will be in direct correlation to the way they are feeling. Considering that someone is "overreacting" to something, when they are clearly upset or distraught, completely invalidates their feelings about the situation and means that the adults supporting them cannot possibly do so effectively.

I like to use "the iceberg theory of behaviour" when considering how someone is acting or behaving. We only see about 10 per cent of an iceberg, the rest is hidden below the waterline. We must remember that what we see regarding an individual's behaviour is being driven by and caused by unseen triggers such as anxiety (which is the biggest trigger with an individual with PDA), sensory needs, social communication differences, hormones, tiredness, hunger etc. If we only address the behaviour of a person without considering what is going on "under the surface" we can never support them adequately with their needs.

When I am speaking to parents and teachers about behaviour that challenges them I often ask them to consider one vital thing: what need is that behaviour fulfilling?

Often behaviour that challenges others is commented on negatively, punished, prevented, sanctioned and sometimes ignored. When we don't meet the underlying need it doesn't just go away. The need continues to exist and may just "pop up" as something different. Sometimes the need grows, silently beneath the surface, until it can no longer be contained. This can result in an explosion of anxiety, anger and distress.

Sometimes as professionals we can get stuck in a game of behaviour "Whack a Mole" which is damaging and exhausting for all concerned.

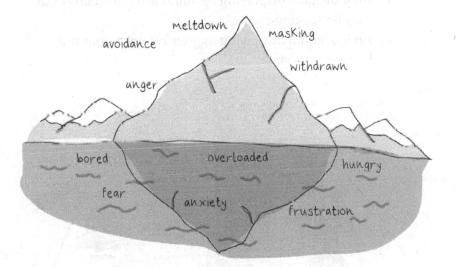

WHAT WE SEE

meltdown

masking

avoidance

withdrawn

unger

bored

overloaded

hungry

fear

anxiety

frustration

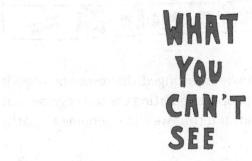

WHAT YOU CAN'T SEE

So think beyond the behaviour and think about what you can do to fulfil that need in a different and more positive and productive way.

- An individual displaying anxiety related behaviour may be seeking trust.
- An individual displaying "attention seeking" behaviour may be seeking connection.
- An individual displaying demand avoidant behaviour may be seeking control.
- An individual displaying aggressive behaviour may be seeking space.

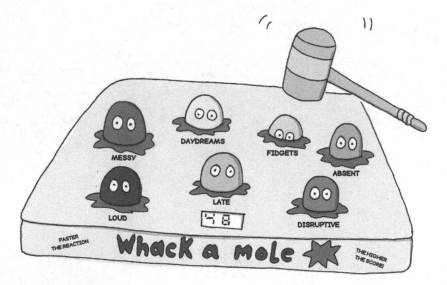

When anyone feels anxious, wronged, distressed or angry it is essential that the people supporting them recognise that their feelings are valid, and that we show genuine empathy at how they feel.

Recently I experienced someone validating my own anxiety and this is a great example of how important it is to do this. Like many people I get anxious about going to the dentist and am lucky that I have found a really lovely dentist who is great with anxious patients.

I particularly dislike the sensation of having my teeth cleaned with the squeaky water jet machine (it probably has a more medical name!). I find it almost unbearable and really, really uncomfortable from a sensory point of view. To me the sensation is similar to that of nails down a blackboard but inside my mouth.

After tolerating the cleaning for about five minutes I had to put my hand up for my dentist to stop as I was finding the squeaky water jet machine intolerable and I just needed a break. At this point the dentist said "I have to white knuckle this too." I was really surprised by this and assumed that, as a dentist, she would be absolutely fine with this procedure. My dentist then continued to say that she hates it too, as does almost everyone, and reassured me that she would stop again if I needed her to.

I instantly felt my anxiety start to dissipate. It found it so reassuring that my dentist genuinely knew how I was feeling and I found the last part of the clean far more bearable as I was more relaxed.

All too often when people are feeling anxious, they are told:

- Calm down.
- It's not that bad.

- You will be fine.
- Don't overreact.
- Stop stressing.
- You were fine last time.
- You will be fine when you get there.

Being told these things does not help to reduce anxiety in any way and will simply leave the individual feeling completely invalidated and even more unsafe and anxious.

Showing true empathy and validation not only reduces anxiety but can also build connections and trust which are so important to neurodivergent individuals.

SHARE THE LOAD

When supporting a learner with PDA with their work, we can show empathy around the things that they find hard. This not only shows that we are validating their feelings but also gives an opportunity for working together which promotes equality and the idea of shared goals that are so important to a learner with PDA.

I have been told on several occasions that there was "no trigger" to an individual having a meltdown or crisis, and I will always disagree with this.

We must remember that the learner with PDA's "anxiety bucket" has probably been slowly filling up over a number of minutes, hours or even days and one tiny last "drop" of anxiety could have been triggered by what is regarded by others as something tiny or irrelevant.

When the anxiety bucket is full this is when an individual with PDA may display behaviours that are labelled as "challenging". In such situations we have to remember that it is the learner who is challenged. Using threats or punishments will only make the situation worse as the individual's anxiety continues to rise and their autonomy is further reduced.

Being told "I understand why you are so angry, worried or upset. I think I would feel that way too" shows an individual that you truly understand and validate their feelings. You could also talk about a time when something similar happened to you, that you felt similar emotions and how you found ways to manage them.

EMPATHISE

I am regularly told by individuals with PDA that, during times of high anxiety, there is one thing that they need – and that is space. Ensuring that a child or young person has a safe space where they can go when they feel overwhelmed is essential in any learning environment. During times of high anxiety it is unlikely that they will ask for this explicitly. It may be communicated through actions such as running away, lashing out or language such as "F**k off!!" or "I hate you – leave me alone!" but it is essential that we respect this need for space and allow the learner to have their time to calm down.

Respecting these wishes will ensure that your connection and trust with the learner are protected, as they should be at all times.

You must also allow yourself time to calm down and reflect after difficult incidents and, if you are in any way responsible for their distress, you should take accountability and apologise. Even just saying "I am sorry I did not understand what you were telling me when you were cross. Next time I will try to do X or Y" shows that you have thought about the situation from your own perspective and are not blaming the learner in any way.

It is also important to remember that "saying sorry" or speaking about an event afterwards will be perceived as a demand. I would always recommend time for both of you to calm down, reflect and heal and then, when the learner is ready, to talk about what happened. Remember that this may takes hours, days or even longer as the individual processes what has happened.

I do not think that an individual should ever be punished or sanctioned for their actions that have been driven by anxiety. Instead of using punishments we should use or talk about "natural consequences". For example, "Mrs Smith is upset because you hit her earlier. She needs some time to feel better so she cannot help you with your LEGO® at the moment" or "The other children don't like it when you tell them what to do all the time, so I think that is why they didn't want to play with you at lunchtime today, but I would like to play with you instead. What shall we do?"

I have found the book *The Incredible 5-Point Scale* by Kari Dunn Burron (2012) a very useful resource over the years to help individuals understand their anxiety better and support them with choices they can make when their anxiety is on the rise.

I have also found story writing very helpful with the children I have worked with. I think "traditional" Social Stories, as created by Carol Gray, can be too directive for a learner with PDA. Instead, I have found using the characters that children like and writing stories about them, weaving in some of the difficulties that the children have experienced and working together to find them solutions can be a really good way of exploring challenges together.

NUMBER	HOW I FEEL	WHAT AM I TRYING TO SAY?

1.

This is easy!
I can handle this!

2.

This is tricky but I can
give it a go.

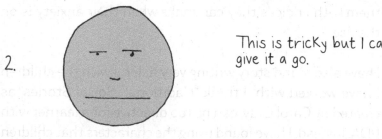

3.

I cannot do this.
I need help.

CHAPTER 14

Choose Your Words Carefully

Learners with PDA will often have extremely well developed language skills, while possibly having difficulties with auditory processing. Some of the children and young people I have worked with have language skills that defy their years.

Remembering at all times that you are working with a child or young person who considers themselves your equal, you should speak to them as such, while always ensuring your language is free of demands and direct instructions. It may feel a bit odd and contrived at first, but I promise you that the more you do it the more natural it will feel.

Let's have a look at some of the demands that were mentioned in the Introduction to this book, oops, actually, that's a demand so I will rephrase it: "I think it may be helpful to have a look at some of the demands outlined in the Introduction to this book."

It is really important to state here that we should never use these approaches to trick or deceive a PDAer into compliance, the examples below are suggestions of ways that we can keep our language as "low demand" as possible:

Direct demands

- Instead of "Sit down" – "Where would you like to sit?"
- Instead of "Start your work" – "Would you like to work with me or have a go on your own?"
- Instead of "Stop talking" – "I wonder if we can work on this quietly for a few minutes?"
- Instead of "Line up now please" – "Would you like to stand at the back of the line or near the front?"

Subtle demands

- Instead of "It's time to start your work now" – "Which task would you like to start on?"
- Instead of "Let's all turn to page seven" – "Shall I find page seven or can you?"
- Instead of "We need to go to assembly now" – "Would you like to go to assembly or would you prefer to stay and help me in the classroom today?"

These are just some examples of how you could adapt your language to support with these demands and expectations and there are many other ways that you could do this.

It can also be effective to "think out loud" when supporting a learner with PDA and talk about the choices that you may make. For example, rather than saying "Put your coat on!", you could explain that you are going to wear your coat so you don't have to waste your valuable breaktime coming inside to retrieve it.

CHAPTER 15

The Importance of Self Care and Looking Out for Each Other

Although it can be great fun and hugely rewarding, working with learners with PDA can also be challenging and tiring at times.

Many sessions with learners with PDA can be met with indifference, refusal or silence. Very often work is not completed or even attempted. This can feel frustrating and even draining and can make you feel flat or deskilled and it can be hard to keep your own enthusiasm levels raised. It is okay to feel this way, but when you are feeling like this it is likely the learner you are supporting will be feeling this too and this could be a sign that you both need a break and a change of pace.

When you support a learner with PDA you must always be aware of their anxiety levels, and constantly adapt and change to meet their needs.

You must be able to pull ideas out of the bag, think on your feet and outside the box.

You may have brilliant ideas which are rejected and rebuffed and it would be easy to feel frustrated by this.

Any anxiety or frustration you feel is likely to be picked up by a learner with PDA, so it is essential that you manage your own emotions effectively.

I also want to tell you that it is okay to make mistakes when you are supporting any learner with complex needs. We all make mistakes; we can learn from them and improve our practice and also role model this with the children and young people we support. I have made many mistakes over the years and I am learning all the time. If things don't go the way I had hoped or expected, then I reflect and think about what I could do better next time.

It is also essential that we support each other in the work-place. On one occasion I arrived at a primary school for a meeting with a lovely LSA who was supporting a boy with PDA. When I met her she was obviously upset, and explained that she had had a very difficult day. The boy she worked with had arrived in school with a "full bucket" and had been unable to enter the classroom or complete any "formal work". Instead, the LSA had spent the entire day in the playground with the child, calming him down and finding natural learning opportunities. The child left much happier at the end of the day, but when this lady went into the staff room for a well-earned break at the end of the day, a colleague had made a loaded comment, saying "Well he's not done much today has he?!" The LSA was so upset that her hard work in keeping the boy calm and safe, as well as the learning that had taken place, had been completely disregarded. No wonder she was upset.

So, look after yourself and each other. Talk about any challenges you are facing with your colleagues and do not be afraid to ask for help when needed.

CHAPTER 16

The Importance of Collaboration – Working with Parents and Other Professionals

During my time in education I have had the pleasure of working with some amazing teachers, LSAs, TAs, therapists and educational and clinical psychologists, and some wonderful parents too.

There are several schools that have done incredible work with learners with PDA, where they have simply thrived. In all these cases there has been a common dominator, and that is that there has been a fantastic, respectful, equal and **collaborative** approach that has involved all the education staff, other professionals and parents.

Everyone has their own area of expertise; teachers are experts in education, therapists and psychologists etc. are experts in their chosen field, and it is essential we recognise that parents are the experts in their own children.

Regular meetings and communication are essential when supporting a learner with PDA. During such meetings everyone's voices and opinions are listened to and are considered of equal importance and validity. Where I have seen the most success is where everyone works together with the child's needs at the heart of everything.

The child is the most important person in their own educational journey, and we should do everything we can together to make it as successful a ride as possible and help them meet their destination.

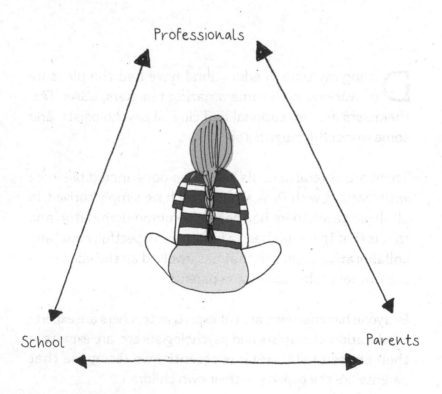

A Quick One-Minute Reminder Guide

Now that you have finished reading the book, this guide will act as a helpful, brief summary of the key points you need to remember when supporting learners with PDA.

- **Remember that ANXIETY is what drives the behaviour of an individual with PDA.** If you always consider the anxiety rather than the behaviour you are more likely to look for solutions and try to help. Also remember that sometimes anxiety stops individuals with PDA doing the things they want to do as well as the things they don't.
- **Use a flexible, non-directive approach.** Use phrases such as "I wonder how we might", "I wonder if this will work if we do it like this?"
- **Be aware of your nonverbal language.** Individuals with PDA can be hypersensitive to tone of voice and facial expressions and body language, which can often cause them increased anxiety as they may misinterpret what you mean, or pick up on the very subtle clues you are giving about the way you are feeling.

- **Offer choices.** This gives the learner greater autonomy and can help to lower anxiety and help the learner feel that they have some control. Examples include "Would you like to do X or Y first?", "Would you like to sit here or here to do your work?"
- **Use challenges, games and races.** "I bet you can't finish this work before me!" Make sure you are joining in these genuinely so that the end result becomes a shared goal.
- **Praise indirectly.** Let them hear you talking about them in a positive way. Don't praise their work directly but elements of their work that you like: "Oh, I really like the colour/wording you have used there, it helps me to understand it better."
- **Use areas of interest to engage and motivate.** Look for ways to weave hobbies and interests into work without hijacking or tainting them.
- **Reduce pressures and pick your battles.** There will be days when anxiety is too high for an individual to cope with any demands. This is fine. You will have good and bad days. Look for ways you can support so demands are decreased, autonomy is increased and anxiety remains as low as possible.
- **Have a sense of humour!** Be prepared to take the mickey out of yourself and make every learning opportunity as fun and engaging as possible.
- **Depersonalise rules.** "I am afraid you can't go outside as its slippery and our Health and Safety rules forbid it" or "It's the law, but I know it is really annoying!"
- **Show empathy.** "I know you find maths really hard. I do too. Shall we work on this together?"

- **Try to find a balance between routine and spontaneity.** This will be dependent on the individual's mood and anxiety levels. But lots of individuals with PDA like surprise and novelty and don't like routine if too rigid or set by others as this feels like a demand.
- **Rewards need to be individualised, quick and personalised.** Often group rewards are ineffective and don't motivate the individual with PDA. You need to make sure they are motivational and change regularly and remember that a reward chart or system is unlikely to support a learner with PDA. Rather than having planned rewards, use natural, positive consequences such as "It's great you have finished this, it means you have time to go on the computer now!"
- **Most importantly! Remember that everyone with PDA is different and should be treated with an individual approach!**

References

American Psychiatric Association (2013) *Diagnostic and Statistical Manual of Mental Disorders, Fifth Edition (DSM-5)*. Washington, DC: American Psychiatric Publishing.

Burron, R.D. (2012) *The Incredible 5-Point Scale: The Significantly Improved and Expanded Second Edition: Assisting Students in Understanding Social Interactions and Controlling Their Emotional Responses*. Shawnee, KS: AAPC Publishing.

PDA Society (n.d.) Home page. Accessed on 21/09/2022 at www.pdasociety.org.uk.

PDA Society (2019, May 14) *Demand Avoidance of the PDA Kind* [Video]. YouTube. Accessed on 21/09/2022 at https://www.youtube.com/watch?v=CCsfRxyuH1I&t=118s.

World Health Organization (2022) International Statistical Classification of Diseases and Related Health Problems (ICD) Version 11. Accessed on 14/11/2022 at https://www.who.int/standards/classifications/classification-of-diseases.

Further Reading

Phil Christie, Margaret Duncan, Zara Healy and Ruth Fidler (2011) *Understanding Pathological Demand Avoidance Syndrome in Children: A Guide for Parents, Teachers and Other Professionals*. London: Jessica Kingsley Publishers.

Ruth Fidler and Phil Christie (2018) *Collaborative Approaches to Learning for Pupils with PDA: Strategies for Education Professionals*. London: Jessica Kingsley Publishers.

Naomi Fisher (2021) *Changing our Minds – How Children Can Take Control of Their Own Learning*. London: Robinson.

Eliza Fricker (2021) *The Family Experience of PDA*. London: Jessica Kingsley Publishers.

Clare Truman (2021) *The Teacher's Introduction to Pathological Demand Avoidance: Essential Strategies for the Classroom*. London: Jessica Kingsley Publishers.